The History of Gawdy Hall & Its Occupants
Redenhall, Norfolk

Including a Snap-shot of Estate Operations in the mid 20th Century

by Rachel Klausner

Foreword by Louis de Bernières

FCS DesignWorks

The History of Gawdy Hall & Its Occupants
Including A Snap-shot of Estate Operations in the mid 20th Century

Published by FCS DesignWorks
Manor Farm
Denton
Harleston
Norfolk IP20 0AX
www.fcsdesignworks.com

Copyright © 2007 by Rachel Klausner

All rights reserved, including the right to reproduce this book or portions thereof, in any form whatsoever.

Printed in England by Barnwell's
Penfold Street
Aylsham
Norfolk NR11 6ET
www.barnwellprint.co.uk

ISBN 978-0-9553969-2-2

Index

Page (i)	Foreword, by Louis de Bernières
Page 1	Introduction
Page 1	Acknowledgements
Page 2	A Brief History of the Gawdy Family

Occupants in Chronological Order

Page 6	1570 – 1583	Thomas Gawdy (vi) of Weybread
Page 8	1583 – 1588	Sir Thomas Gawdy (v) of Claxton
Page 13	1588 – 1622	Lady Frances Gawdy
Page 14	1622 – 1629	Lady Mary Gawdy
Page 16	1629 – 1661	Sir Thomas Gawdy (vii)
Page 17	1661 – 1662	William Gawdy
Page 18	1662 – 1666	Tobias Frere
Page 19	1666 – 1707	Sarah Frere & John Wogan
Page 20	1707 – 1778	John Wogan (ii) & John Wogan (iii)
Page 23	1778 – 1796	Revd Gervas Holmes (ii)
Page 27	1796 – 1831	John Holmes
Page 30	1831 – 1849	William Sancroft Holmes
Page 31	1849 – 1869	Hester Sancroft Holmes
Page 32	1869 – 1920	John Sancroft Holmes
Page 36	1920 – 1937	Edith Sancroft Holmes
Page 37	1938 –	The Tresfon family, present owners
Page 38		Transcript of the original sale documents detailing the house and gardens

Page 51	Farming Operations on the Estate in the Mid 20th Century
Page 64	Livestock on the Estate
Page 67	Brief History of the Inner Temple
Page 68	Sir John Soane, Architect
Page 69	Arms of Gawdy

Foreword

There is no shortage of histories on the subjects of nations, battles, and great men, as if history were not something inside of which the entire human race has always lived, even those humble souls who were born into a village and never left it until the day of their death. These days we find that there is a need and demand for other kinds of history. Genealogy is no longer a subject for the diversion of aristocrats, and people are prepared to travel from continent to continent in search of gravestones, distant relatives and ancient ties. The visitors' book in Denton Church is a vivid illustration of this, and I have had people call in at my house in order to see where their family lived in the eighteenth century.

Parallel with this, there is a growing interest in local history, and we no longer mock old people who keep going on about the old days, because nowadays we all want to know what it was like. It may be that this is a result of reduced optimism about the future, but on the other hand it is not merely nostalgia for a golden age that really was not very comfortable. No-one seriously wants to return to a time when people routinely died of appendicitis or tetanus, and you had to hand over one tenth of all your produce to the rector. I think the truth is that most of us have a deepseated need to feel that we belong somewhere, and getting to know a place's history is part of the process of learning to be more at home in it.

Perhaps the one thing that has changed more than anything else in the English countryside is the role of the great houses and great estates. They were the motor of rural economies, providing a huge proportion of the necessary employment. Quite apart from the servants of both sexes, estates would need teams of gardeners, carpenters and maintenance personnel, as well as tenant farmers, farm labourers and gamekeepers. It is impossible to know exactly what proportion of landowners were beneficent and enlightened, but I have heard of one who built a wall around his entire estate in order to give gainful work to local people who would otherwise have been living in penurious unemployment. The great houses were training grounds for all sorts of trades, from cook to farrier, and their families provided a role model, for good or ill, to those of humbler origin who wanted to better themselves.

I think that the great houses and estates vanished for several reasons. One was the consequence of the Great War, which, as every village war memorial attests, removed entire sets of brothers from the face of the earth. Many estates lost their heirs, and when there is a shortage of skilled and unskilled labour, the wages go up, and a large workforce becomes less feasible. The Great War did terrible damage to our economy, and the great families were becoming steadily poorer. Increasing industrialisation was attracting labour to the cities, and the mechanisation of farming was effectively driving it out of the countryside in any case. Rural England was emptying out, and it is still much emptier than it used to be. Vast numbers of people had gone to serve or work in farflung parts of the Empire – my great uncles and one grandfather were all in India, where one died of cholera – and no-one had yet realised that the Empire was making a massive financial loss, the cheap raw materials never paying us back for the investment in infrastructure, bureaucracy, and military capacity.

A second heavy blow to the countryside was inheritance tax, in the view of this writer a vindictive act of class warfare by chippy townies who hoped thereby to destroy the economic base of the gentry. It certainly worked, and many estates had to be broken up and sold off. Anecdotal evidence suggests that a very large number of great houses were demolished in order to avoid the tax, and that this practise continued unchecked until the system of listing came into being. In any case, most of the great houses had been built a long time in the past, and were now desperately in need of renovation. The Adairs at Flixton Hall were just one family who found that it was simply impossible to find the money to repair their vast rambling building, and now their former estate has become a series of gravel pits.

Similarly, the family at Gawdy Hall found that they could not afford to replace the entire roof, and that was the end of that.

Despite the lack of a hall, the Gawdy Estate still exists and functions, and its gardens have been preserved. Rachel Klausner carefully traces the arc of its history and of those who have lived and worked there, be they lawyer or lunatic. In here you will find much fascinating information, such as the value of a secondhand Caterpillar tractor in 1950, and how timber was harvested and sawn every new year. There is interesting documentation, such as the proclamation of Robert Fellowes to his workers in December 1830, or the Kirby Cane tithe book entry for 1628, and there is plenty of entertaining anecdote, such as the one concerning Sir Francis Gawdy, who had turned his own parish church into a dog kennel and hayloft, and therefore had nowhere to be buried when he died.

Rachel Klausner comes from a local farming family of long standing, and is one the those astoundingly creative and intelligent people who is one minute making vases on a lathe, then playing the flute, and then painting on glass. This work is her most ambitious project yet, although I suspect that there will be yet more ambitious ones to come. Readers will find here a substantial contribution to local historiography, and I have no doubt that this new and expanded edition will be even more successful that the last one.

Louis de Bernières, Denton, September 2007

Introduction

The Gawdys, a family of lawyers, flourished in Norfolk and Suffolk in the sixteenth and seventeenth centuries. The true fortunes of this family were founded in the Tudor period by the remarkable genius of three half-brothers who rose to positions of prominence in the legal profession.

The eldest, Thomas Gawdy, Sergeant-at-Law became Recorder of Norwich and Lynn; the second, Sir Thomas Gawdy became Justice of the Queen's Bench; and the third, Sir Francis Gawdy became Justice of the Common Pleas.

The influence of these three great lawyers lent considerable prestige to the name of Gawdy, and brought the family into close contact with prominent figures and affairs of state.

The family correspondence and papers, known as The Gawdy Family Papers, which chiefly concern the main, or West Harling branch are currently in the British Library consisting of over 5,000 documents. A narrative of the lives of two 17th century deaf brothers created out of letters and other family documents. They are considered of great genealogical, historical and literary value.

Acknowledgements
This book would not have been possible without the help and assistance of John and Rosie Fearnley, Robert and Sarah Fearnley, David Green, Alan Oakley, John Spurdens and Paul Seligman.

Thanks must also go to Mrs Tresfon, Lady Darrell, Marion Folkes, The Soane Museum, Norfolk Record Office and Percy Millican's 1939 publication regarding the Gawdy family.

To Andrew, Alex & Philip.

A Brief History of the Gawdy Family

Originally French in origin, the first documented Gawdy to arrive on British soil was Sir Brews Gawdy, a French Knight taken prisoner in 1352, who became naturalised and settled in Suffolk. Sir Brews Gawdy married a daughter of William Hammond of Swaffham Bulbeck in Cambridgeshire where the family resided for about a century. In the fifteenth century, a branch of the family settled in Norfolk. On 27th January 1459, Robert Gawdy (i), senior, of Redenhall, executed his will, which was proved three weeks later. He ordered his body to be buried at Redenhall and mentions his wife Catharine, to whom he gave the life enjoyment of all his lands and tenements in Redenhall. Robert (i) had three sons; Robert (ii), Thomas (i) and John (i).

The eldest son Robert (ii) died in 1467, leaving his widow Catharine (daughter of John Peck) and a son, William (d. 1491). William married Joan (daughter of Robert Lenrick) and had two sons, both named Thomas. Thomas (ii) (d. 1543), the oldest brother being of Wortwell and the younger brother Thomas (iii) (b. c1476 d. 1556), of Harleston.

Robert Gawdy's (i) youngest son John lived with his wife Alice at the Priory Manor in Mendham, Suffolk. Alice died before her husband and they did not have any children. John died in 1510 and was buried near to his wife in Redenhall Church. In the middle alley of the north chapel was formerly a Latin inscription on a stone under the portraitures of John and Alice Gawdy.

William's eldest son Thomas (ii) of Wortwell married twice but did not have any children. His second wife was Agnes (d. 1544) (daughter of Thomas Tower, hardwareman of Halesworth and stallholder on Norwich market. Agnes' brother Simon Tower, was citizen and mercer of Norwich). By his will, Thomas (ii) ordered to be buried near his mother and father and his first wife in Redenhall Church.

He gave Agnes the enjoyment of his estate so long as she remained his widow. The inquisition after his death was taken at Stowmarket on 6th November 1542 and states that his brother Thomas (iii) Gawdie of Harleston was his next heir.

The younger of the two brothers, Thomas (iii) was described as Bailiff of Harleston in John Gawdy's will of 1509. He married three times:-

The first marriage was to Elizabeth Hellows (or Helwise), by whom a son Thomas (iv) was born who became Sergeant-at-Law of Shotesham and Norwich. From him sprang the Harling branch of the Gawdy family.

The second marriage was to Rose of Shotesham Hall (daughter of Thomas Bennett of Rushall). Rose and Thomas (iii) had a daughter Margaret and another son called Thomas (v) who became Sir Thomas Gawdy of Claxton.

The third marriage was to Elizabeth (daughter of Thomas (or Oliver) Shires), by whom another son named Thomas was born (known as Francis to differentiate him from the other Thomases in the family!) He went on to become Chief Justice of the Common Pleas.

Thomas Gawdy (iii) of Harleston was thus the progenitor of the three great branches of the family in East Anglia. His will is dated 12th August 1556 – just eight days after his first son's death. By it, he ordered his body to be buried at Redenhall near his first wife, and mentions his house called Menes house (now known as Reydon House in Harleston). The will also mentions daughters Elizabeth Southall and Catherine Gawdy. He bequeathed to his wife Elizabeth the enjoyment for life of his Estate; and his sons Thomas (v) and Francis whom he made executors. In documents dated 14th January 1556 it is stated that in 1533 he was worth £100 a year. His widow Elizabeth was buried at Redenhall in 1563. Her will mentions her daughter Margaret Aldrich; her grandchild Catharine Southall, her god-child Elizabeth Gawdy;

her daughter Catharine Gawdy (whom she made executrix) and her sons Thomas (v) and Francis, supervisors.

The eldest son Thomas Gawdy (iv) of Shotesham, Redenhall and Norwich, was mentioned in the inquisition following the death of his uncle, Thomas (ii) Gawdy of Wortwell in 1533 as being worth £40 a year.

Thomas (iv) entered the Inner Temple* where he was Lent reader in 1548 and 1553 and was fined for refusing to read in the latter year. In 1545 he became Recorder of King's Lynn, and in 1547 was M.P. for that town.

There was much civil unrest in England at this time, with elevated inflation and rising unemployment. In the villages common lands were enclosed by local squires for grazing sheep, reducing to the rank of land-less labourers or vagrants many of the poorer peasants who relied on them for their own income. Against this background a dispute over church property in the Norfolk town of Wymondham in the summer of 1549 exploded into full scale revolt. Norwich, the second city of England, was sacked with 20,000 rebels encamped within its walls and over 4,000 people dead. Thomas Gawdy (iv) became involved when he was imprisoned at Surrey House - the temporary headquarters of Robert Kett, a yeoman farmer who was the rioters ring-leader. Thomas (iv) and the small group of fellow prisoners escaped on August 26th when the King's Army, made up of men from London, Essex and Suffolk and headed by the Earl of Warwick, attacked the rebels who had retreated to the Dussingdale estate at Thorpe. Kett finally surrendered and was later hanged from Norwich Castle.

The following year in 1550 Thomas (iv) was elected Recorder of Norwich and at the same time was given the freedom of the City. He held the office of Recorder until his death. In 1552, he was promoted to Sergeant-at-Law, and in 1553 represented Norwich in Parliament.

*A brief history of the Inner Temple is on Page 67.

In 1554 he was one of a Royal Commission appointed to inquire into a conspiracy in Norfolk in connection with Queen Mary.

A ring, which was commissioned in 1552 by *'Thomas Gawdy of Shotesham'*, was found in 1977 at St Mary's Priory, Coxford (it is now in the Lynn Museum). It is a gold finger ring with the inscription PLEBS SINE LEGER VIT+, meaning *'people without law are destroyed'*, which was the motto adopted by a group of Sergeants-at-Law called in 1552 - Robert Brooke, Richard Catelyn, William Dalison, James Dyer, Thomas Gawdy, Ralph Rokeby and William Staunford.

Thomas Gawdy (iv) married three times:-

The first marriage was to Anne (daughter of John Bassingborne of Hatfield, Herts) by whom he had two sons, Thomas (vi) (b. 1531) and Bassingborne, and a daughter Catharine.

The second was to Elizabeth (daughter of John Harris of Radford, near Plymouth). Two sons, Anthony and John were borne of this marriage.

The third marriage was to Catharine (daughter of Robert Lestrange). They did not have any children together.

1570 – 1583
Thomas (vi) of Weybread

Thomas Gawdy of Weybread (vi), the eldest son of Thomas (iv) and Anne married Honor (daughter of Walter Staynings of Honycott, Somerset). In 1569 their daughter Catharine married Edward Bacon of Harleston who was lord of Holbrook Manor in Redenhall, which formerly belonged to the Turbervilles and Tyndales. In 1570, Thomas (vi) purchased his son-in-law's manor and at about this period the ancient mansion called Holbrook was demolished and the building, which has ever since been known as Gawdy Hall, was erected.

c1570 Thomas (vi) petitioned to be excused lending the Queen 100 marks on privy seal, alleging that he had lent the late Queen £10 which had not been repaid. He declared that he had since been at great charge in building, having borrowed from friends and others 1,000 marks to complete a purchase and the said building, and to support his wife and many children. The building to which he refers is certainly Gawdy Hall.

In 1568 Christopher Watson dedicated a book to his host, *'the right worshipful Thomas Gaudy, esq From my chamber in your house at Gaudy Hall, Norfolk'*. This black leather-bound book was found in Mr Gervas Holmes' (future owner of Gawdy Hall) possession entitled, Histories of the Worthy Chronographer, Polybius, published in 1568.

At around 1580 Thomas (vi) was involved in lawsuits and suffered considerable losses, which compelled him in 1583 to sell the Manor of Redenhall to his uncle Sir Thomas Gawdy (v) of Claxton. Sir Thomas (v) appears to have been mortgagee of the Gawdy Estates as early as 1576, although the final conveyance was not executed until 1583.

Thomas (vi) then retired to his only remaining property in East Anglia, Weybread Hall, and died c1595, his wife Honor surviving him.

The will of Nicholas Hare of Stow Bardolph in 1596 contains an interesting request:-

"I give to Mrs Honor Gawdie, widoe, one hundred and thirty pounds yearly during her life ... which I think myselfe bound in conscience to give unto her for that she by my persuasion released unto Sir Thomas Gawdye, Knight, all her title of dower in the lands which the said Sir Thomas purchased of her husband, in consideration whereof the said Sir Thomas promised to deale liberalie with her, but in dede performed nothinge."

Honor died in 1601. Her grandson Henry Gawdy of Weybread parted with the Weybread estate to Elizabeth de la Fontaine. In 1603 he was in an impoverished condition, and in 1627/28 was in a debtor's prison – the Wood Street Counter, London. As this branch of the family sank deeper into poverty, its members became dependent on their more wealthy relations.

1583 – 1588
Sir Thomas Gawdy (v) of Claxton

Sir Thomas Gawdy (v) of Claxton and Redenhall, the only son of Thomas (iii) and Rose entered Cambridge University and is described as a matriculation pensioner from Trinity Hall in 1545. He was admitted to the Inner Temple 12th February 1549/50; bencher, 1551, being then one of the masters of request; M.P. for Arundel in 1553.

After the death of his father and brother in 1556, he was designated *Thomas Gawdy, senior, esquire,* in order to distinguish him from his nephew, Thomas (vi) Gawdy of Redenhall and Weybread. In August 1556 he was elected Steward of Norwich and made honorary freeman of the city on the death of his predecessor Richard Catelyn. He resigned this position in 1557, when he was elected M.P. for Norwich, and in 1558 was summoned to graduate as Sergeant-at-Law. In 1558 he was elected recorder of Norwich. From 1561 to 1564, Thomas (v) was treasurer of the Inner Temple and in 1562, treasurer of Lincoln's Inn. He reached the zenith of his legal career on 16th November 1574, when he was constituted Judge of the Queen's Bench and was one of the few powerful judges of the time to receive the honour of knighthood from Queen Elizabeth. He was knighted at Woodrising on 26th August 1578, on the occasion of the Queen's visit to Norfolk, and in the record of his knighthood he is described as *of Gawdy Hall.* Although he was mortgagee of the Hall at that time, records show that he did not take final possession until 1583. It is believed that Queen Elizabeth stayed at Gawdy Hall during her Norfolk visit.

Sir Thomas (v) sat as a Judge for fourteen years and played a leading part in many famous trials. He was one of the commission which tried Mary, Queen of Scots in 1586, and of that which had tried her supporter, Dr William Parry, the notorious intriguer the previous year.

In his capacity of Recorder of Norwich his name frequently appears in the city records. Among the important local trials at which both he and his half-brother, Francis, officiated as Judges, were those which took place at Norwich in 1584, when a great many persons were charged with recusancy (refusing to obey the Church of England) and disobedience of the ordinances relating to religious observances. He was also one of the commission appointed in 1578 to enquire into the violent quarrel which had arisen between Edmund Freke, Bishop of Norwich and the Chancellor, John Beacon.

His legal arguments are reported by Sir James Dyer, Edmund Plowden and Sir Edward Coke – the last, of whom was his nephew by marriage, describing him as *"a most reverend Judge and sage of the law, of ready and profound judgement and venerable gravity, prudence and integrity."* But a merciless and grasping side of his character is revealed in the acquisition of Gawdy Hall from his Nephew, Thomas (vi), whose widow Honor, mentioned previously, was left in dire poverty, regardless of definite promises to the contrary.

Sir Thomas (v) married twice;-

Firstly to Etheldreda (or Audrey), daughter and co-heiress of William Knightley, attorney-at-law of Norwich in 1548.

Secondly to Frances, daughter of Henry Richers of Swannington, Norwich in 1567.

The property at Rockland, Bramerton and Surlingham which came into his possession as a result of his first marriage formed the nucleus of the very large estate which rapidly accumulated during his lifetime. c1549, Sir Thomas (v) purchased the manor of Holveston from the co-heiress of William Halse of Haveringland.

On his retirement from the treasurership of the Inner Temple in November 1564, he sought a more imposing residence in Norfolk, and in that year commenced negotiations for the purchase of John Throckmerton's estates, which included the manors of Claxton and Hellington. Throckmerton at this time appears to have been one of the creditors of Thomas Gawdy (vi) at Gawdy Hall, so when Sir Thomas (v) came into final possession of most of the Throckmerton estates in 1565/6, he also took John Throckmerton's place as an important creditor of his nephew and namesake.

From around 1558 until 1567, he hired a newly-built house in St Giles, Norwich. In 1567 he purchased from his nephew Anthony Gawdy (son of his half-brother Thomas (iv)), a large house in St Julian's Parish in Norwich, which his half-brother had used during his Recordership of the city.

Etheldreda (or Audrey), Sir Thomas' (v) first wife died c1566. By this marriage there were three sons; Sir Henry, Thomas (vii) and George, and four daughters; Isabel who married John Mingay of Norwich, Anne who married Thomas Reade of Weston, Suffolk, Mary who married Sir Isaac Wyncoll, and Frances who married Sir Edmund Moundeford of Feltwell.

Following the death of his first wife, Sir Thomas (v) subsequently married Frances, daughter of Henry Richers of Swannington in 1567. Sir Thomas (v) had conducted a considerable amount of business in real estate in his younger days with her family. They had a second family of which Sir Clippesby Gawdy was the only son. This second marriage supplied the money with which the Redenhall and neighbouring estates were purchased – Gawdy Hall at this time was in the process of being built.

Sir Thomas (v) was unquestionably one of the greatest legal authorities of his time. Although he did not attain the senior office of Chief Justice to which his half-brother Francis was promoted, or the literary distinction which made his relative, Sir Edward Coke, famous, yet his name still appears in many national and local records – a fact which bears witness to his widespread official activities and to the respect and confidence which his profound learning earned for his judgement.

On the other hand we find evidence in the family records of strained relations existing between him and the Harling branch of the family. Undoubtedly caused by jealousy of his succession and especially by the unforgivable purchase by him, a junior member of the family, of the paternal estate at Redenhall.

Sir Thomas (v) died on 5th November 1588 at Gawdy Hall and was buried the following 12th December in the family chapel in Redenhall Church where an alter-tomb without inscription is said to mark his last resting place. An amount of 6s. 8d was received for his grave.

The date of Sir Thomas' (v) burial coincided with that of the marriage of his nephew, Bassingborne Gawdy to Margaret Sulyard; *"so that on that day members of the family had the choice of wearing mourning or holiday attire as they felt inclined."*

At his death he was succeeded on the Bench by his half-brother, Sir Francis Gawdy.

Sir Francis Gawdy, as a Judge, took part in several State Trials, namely, the Earl of Arundel on 18th April 1589, Sir John Perrot in June 1592, Robert Devereux, Earl of Essex, in June 1600. He was one of the Advisors to the peers in Essex's trial for high treason in February 1601 and Sir Walter Raleigh in November 1603, as to which he is stated to have said on his death-bed that *"the justice of England was never so depraved and injured as in the condemnation of Sir Walter Raleigh."*

Sir Francis died suddenly of apoplexy at Sergeant's Inn and was buried at Runcton, Norfolk, in the following year. *"Having made his appropriate Parish church, a hay-house or dog-kennel, his dead corpse, being brought from London to Wallirigton, could for many days find no place of burial, but in the meantime growing very offensive by the contagious and ill savours that issued through the chinks of lead, not well soldered, he was at last carried to a poor church of a little village thereby called Runcton and brined there without any ceremony."*

1588 – 1622
Lady Frances Gawdy

Sir Thomas' (v) widow, Lady Frances Gawdy, continued her residency at Gawdy Hall where she died in 1622 having survived him for thirty-four years.

She also survived their only son, Sir Clippesby Gawdy who died on 17th December 1619 at the age of 45 years.

1622 – 1629
Lady Mary Gawdy

Upon Lady Frances' death, Gawdy Hall passed to Sir Clippesby's widow, Lady Mary Gawdy who was bequeathed the Redenhall Estate for her life, with remainder to Sir Clippesby Gawdy's son, Thomas (vii).

By her first husband, William Brews, Lady Mary had several children. She died in 1629. She asked her son-in-law Edmond Moundeford, in her will, dated 24th December 1628, *"to have the guardianship of her son Thomas Gawdy (vii), according to the desire of his grandmother, Lady Frances Gawdy, deceased. The said Thomas to have £200 a year during his minority."*

In 1625 an exceptionally fine star-shaped watch was made. It is signed on the backplate "David Ramsay Scotus me fecit" (David Ramsay Scotus made me) and on the dial "de Heck sculp". It is an exceptionally fine specimen of the work of the artisan who was clockmaker to James I and Charles I. It is said that this, along with two apostle spoons and some Jacobean manuscripts were hidden at the time of the Civil War. They were recovered c1790 in a recess behind the tapestry, which then covered the walls in the dining room at Gawdy Hall.

The watch has biblical scenes engraved inside and outside the covers and the edges of the points of the star are decorated with engravings of wild animals. (See page 31).

This is now displayed in the Clockmakers' Museum in London's historic Guildhall.

The tithe account book (1619-1712) of the rectors of Kirby Cane, Norfolk, contains a rental of the estate at Redenhall at the time of the death of Lady Mary Gawdy. This record was made by Thomas Potts, rector of Kirby Cane, 1619-1646:-

A particular of Rednall cum Halston. Novem. 28, 1628.

The lady Gaudies 60 milch cowes; gastreard (calves fostered by heifers) calves tyth 5; low meddow, 20 acr.; hardlond meddow, 30 acr.; pastur fed with fat ware, 20 acr.; lambs tyth, 6; wooll, 2 stone; hemp of 2 bushell seed; hopps; rabbets, pigeons, turkeys, geese; plowd land, 100 acr.; underwoods tythable, 120 acr. ... £200.

Her fearmers:
Will. Thompson (£50), Thomas Fuller (£50), John Wright (£40), Thomas Hynes (£10), Sygismund Skeet (£4), John Clerk (£16), John Hanner (£28), John Pauley (£2), Lyonell Caer (£30), RobertGower (£16), Mr. Hammond Ward (£80), Thomas Selwyn (£60), Edmund Germie (£10), - Warne (£8), John Burgesse (£16), Elmham Town (£8), Mr. John Holland (£80), John Chalker (£70), - Freeman (£16), Robt. Tibnam (£4), Will. Stanton (£6), Widdow Emmat (£6), Richard Say (£30), Ralph Fuller (£8), Steeven Churchfield (£20), - Germie (£15), - Cooper (£18), Thomas Corbold (£50), Will. Cook (£30), Henry Woolnough (£10), Mr. Grudgefeild (£10), Mr. Burley (£20), John Corbold (£8), Mr. Baxter (£200), Thomas Fuller (£20), Mr. Freer (£80), Thomas Corbyn (£5), John Westgat (£6), Mr. Wiseman (£10), Mr. Cotton (£50), Nicn. Cook (£5), Mr. Wales (£50), Widdow Allen (£10), Francis Galard (£12), Henry Skeet (£2), Rich. Corbyn, St James (£2), Thomas Wakfeild (£2), Arthur Carter (£5), Rich. Corbyn, alb. (£2), Marie Baker (£2), Franciss Garold (£2), Rob. Welton (£2), Will. Garold (£2), Mr. Barnard (£6), - Hall (£1). Withowse pictle (£3), The closes between the wayes, hidd (£4).

Gleabs in possession, 30 acr.; more to be recovered, 30 acr.; obventions and oblations, £7; diet tythes, £5; tytheing of cottengers, £4; root grownds, £1; the howse and orchard, £4.3

1629 – 1661
Sir Thomas Gawdy (vii)

Thomas Gawdy (vii) of Gawdy Hall (b. c1610) was the only surviving child of Sir Clippesby Gawdy. He was admitted at Corpus Christi College, Cambridge in 1625 and at Grays Inn, 1627.

In May 1629 he married Anne, daughter of Sir William Spring at Pakenham, and by her had a number of physically weak children. William Gawdy, the eldest son was born c1631. Charles Gawdy, the second surviving son was baptized in Redenhall Church in 1642. In December 1629 Thomas (vii) was knighted, although apparently he was mentally unstable.

In 1634 he wrote to his previous guardian, Sir Edmund Moundeford desiring the appointment of Captain of Foot. Sir Edmund, writing to Framlingham Gawdy of Harling remarked that, although in his opinion the post was not worth having, yet *"it may be a means to bring him* (Sir Thomas (vii)) *to Gawdy Hall and a more stayed brain."*

The tremendous upheaval of the Civil War reduced him and many others of that time to poverty. In 1643 he was a member of the Committee of the Associated Counties, which had been appointed for the disposal of forces and for the collection of funds. In 1645 his name appears in the overseers Account Book for Redenhall as owner and occupier of Gawdy Hall.

In 1646, his wife, Lady Anne Gawdy was buried in Redenhall and in 1654 Sir Thomas (vii) was in a state of severe financial depression.

1661 – 1662
William Gawdy

Sir Thomas' (vii) oldest son, William, was admitted to Corpus Christ College, Cambridge in 1647. His name is mentioned in the settlement (1632) by which the Chapel of St. John at Harleston was vested in trustees for the benefit of the inhabitants.

In 1661 Thomas Elliott petitioned the King *"for the custody of the body and estates of William Gaudy of Gaudy Hall, Norfolk, a lunatic, his near relations not having petitioned for his custody."*

Charles Gawdy, Sir Thomas' (vii) second son appears to have been responsible for the final sale of Gawdy Hall, probably owing to the insanity of his older brother, William.

Thus the Gawdy's of Claxton and Redenhall who survived the Restoration, having lost the estates which they had enjoyed for nearly a century, were forced by circumstances to descend to a lower social plane, and all connections with the Estate, which still bears their family name over four centuries later, ended.

1662 – 1666
Tobias Frere Snr & his Son Tobias

The Gawdy Hall Estate was subsequently mortgaged by Tobias Frere, a noted attorney in the Harleston district and owner of Caltofts – a large estate situated in the centre of Harleston.

It is stated in Redenhall Parish Accounts by Mr Candler of Harleston, that *"Tobias Frere was an attorney of good means"*. In 1654 he was a Justice of the Peace, Sequestrator and M.P. for Norfolk. He died in 1655, leaving a widow Susanna, and a son Tobias who went on to purchase Gawdy Hall outright in c1662.

Tobias Frere, the new Lord of the Manor, married Sarah Longe (b. c1639, d. 1684 - she was the daughter of Robert Longe of Foulden, who was Sheriff of Norfolk in 1644).

From this marriage there were two children, Tobias and Elizabeth, both of whom died in childhood. Tobias died in 1666.

1666 – 1707
Sarah Frere & John Wogan

Tobias' widow Sarah thus inherited Gawdy Hall. She subsequently married John Wogan (b. 1632, d. c1707), the kinsman of Lewis Wogan of Boulston Castle, Pembrokeshire by license on 31st December 1667 and they resided in Covent Garden, London.

It is not until the following year that John Wogan is recorded as being Lord of the Manor of Redenhall.

John and Sarah had two children, John (ii) (b. c1668) and Walter.

In 1684 Sarah Wogan died and was buried at Redenhall Church.

1707 – 1778
John Wogan (ii) & John Wogan (iii)

Upon his fathers' death, John and Sarah's eldest son John (ii) took over the Estate. John Wogan (ii) had three children, John (iii) (b. 1713, d. 1778), Sarah (ii) (b. c1729) and Elizabeth (b. 1710, d. 1728). John (ii) was brought up to the Bar and was admitted to Gray's Inn on 11th February 1683. He married in 1706 Elizabeth Sancroft, the niece of the celebrated Archbishop of Canterbury, and it appears from the will of his father that provision was made for him and his brother Walter in the settlement on that occasion. Elizabeth Sancroft died in 1755 having survived her husband by several years. In John's (ii) will he left his daughters £1,000 each and lands in Fressingfield and Cratfield, while his brother Walter was given £40.

Between 1713 and 1778 John Wogan (ii) assigned the alteration of the direction of the moat, which bounded the flower garden at the west side of the house. At one period it existed on three sides of the Hall. When he came into possession, John (ii) extended and altered it so as to give it the appearance of a river.

John (iii) succeeded to the Estate and married his cousin Elizabeth (b. 1714, d. 1778), the daughter of William and Catherine Sancroft (Catherine was the daughter of Sir John Hynde Cotton, of Madingley, Cambridge, Receiver for that town - William was the great nephew of Archbishop Sancroft). Elizabeth was ultimately the sole heiress of Francis Sancroft, the grandnephew of the Archbishop and by this marriage properties at Fressingfield were merged into the Estate. They Wed at Gray's Inn Chapel in 1735.

In 1688 the Great Archbishop was sent to the tower (with six other Bishops) for refusing to order the Clergy to read James II's 'Declaration of Indulgence'. Several of his relics remained in the Hall.

Archbishop Sancroft and the Bishops, 1688
Bust of Archbishop Sancroft, wearing a cap and clerically robed. Seven cameo busts of bishops William Lloyd, Francis Turner, John Lake, Henry Compton, Thomas Ken, Thomas White and Sir John Trelawney; a field of stars. By George Bower.

Portrait of Catherine Sancroft and her sister Elizabeth
Signed l.l..: J Maubert

John (iii) and Elizabeth had a son, John (iv) (b.1736, d.1763) and a daughter, Elizabeth (ii) (b. 1755, d. 1773). The latter died unmarried in 1773. Her brother John (iv) died a batchelor in 1763, in his father's lifetime.

John's (ii) daughter, Sarah Wogan (ii) married the Revd Gervas Holmes (b. 1692, d. 1776), vicar of Fressingfield, on 10th April 1740. They had three children; Gervas Holmes (ii) (b. 1741, d. 1796), Sarah Holmes (b. 1742, d. 1742 at 2 months old) and Sarah Holmes (b. 1744, d. 1765). Sarah Wogan (ii) died on the 17th May 1764 aged 55 years.

John Wogan (iii), last of that name at Gawdy Hall, died on 31st May 1778, aged 65, and by his will directed all his Estates to be sold and the proceeds invested. The interest from the investments from this Norfolk property was allotted to his sisters' husband, Revd Gervas Holmes and their children. A legacy to the testator's sister-in-law Catherine Sancroft was also bequeathed to the children of Sir John Hynde Cotton.

1778 – 1796
Revd Gervas Holmes (ii)

Valuation of the Gawdy Hall Estate was carried out in 1779, a year after John Wogan's (iii) death, describing the Hall in great detail with dimensions of rooms (drawing room not finished) with a draft letter offering the Estate to Governor Dalling for £27,000. It showed the acreage being 764a 2r 35p, the annual rent being £562 2s 0d. The timber on the property was valued about three years previously at over £10,000 *"exclusive of a large number of young ash and oak. Since that date, however, a portion of it had been cut down."* These particulars also record that *"At a convenient distance from the House are exceeding good new built Stables for fifteen horses with a Clock Turret over the same; Coach-house for three Carriages; a large Cart Horse Stable, Wagon Shed and other convenient Buildings."* It also mentions *"The Kitchen Garden Walled and planted with variety of fruit trees, together with shrubberies, water, etc."*

The Stables today.

The Estate however, was not sold, and in 1778 Revd Gervas Holmes (ii) who succeeded his father as Vicar of Fressingfield inherited the Estates and entire fortunes of the Wogan and Sancroft families and was bequeathed to take the name and arms of Sancroft.

After his wife Sarah's (ii) death, he married Rebecca (nee Grimwood), then Charlotte Isabella Williams. He died on 28th July 1776 and was buried in St Peter & St Paul's Church, Fressingfield.

In 1788 extensive alterations to the house were made including a new library. The work was carried out under the supervision of Sir John Soane*. The total cost of the work was £951.7.4¼.

Soane's first visit to survey the house was on 4th March 1788 and he made six subsequent visits between then and November 1789, two from nearby houses on which he was also working - Tendring Hall and Shotesham Park.

On 28th March 1788 he sent *"3 fair drawings of a design for alteration per the Norwich Mail : 1 general plan, 1 plan of the ground floor and 3 elevations and 1 plan of the Bed Chamber floor"*. On 10th October he *"sent per Ipswich Mail four drawings for workmen of finishings to Drawing Room and Chamber on 3 sheets of paper"*. On 12th November 1788 he *"sent by post sketch of Privy on letter paper"* and on 16th December 1799 he *"sent by post a drawing for workmen of a design for a bookcase on a sheet of copy paper"*. The drawings of the drawing room chimney piece (see page 25) are currently in the Soane museum, London.

The main portion of the house had at one time a much steeper roof, under which was another storey of apartments. Revd Gervas Holmes (ii), finding the accommodation too large for his requirements, lowered the pitch and reduced the size of the house. It is likely that it was at this time that the Hall took a drastic change in appearance to keep up with current architectural trends.

*A brief outline of Sir John Soane, Architect, is on page 68.

In 1773, Revd Gervas Holmes (ii) married Rebecca Grimwood (b. c1743) by license in Dedham, Essex. They had three children, John Holmes (b. 1774, d. 1831), Gervas Holmes (iii) (b. 1776) and Rebecca Holmes (b. 1778).

View of the Hall from the east.

View of the west side of the Hall from across the moat.

1796 – 1831
John Holmes

John Holmes was heir to the Gawdy Hall Estate along with Fressingfield Hall following his father, Revd Gervas Holmes' (ii) death.

John was Justice of the Peace for Norfolk, Rector and Vicar of St Mary's, Flixton in 1814, and between 1820 and 1831 was Rector of All Saints and St Nicholas, South Elmham.

He married Anne Whitear (b. 1784) on 21st April 1812 in Starston and had three children; William Sancroft Holmes (b. 1815 d. 1849), Anna Holmes (b. 1817) and Charlotte Holmes (b. 1819).

John died in Gawdy Hall on 29th April 1831.

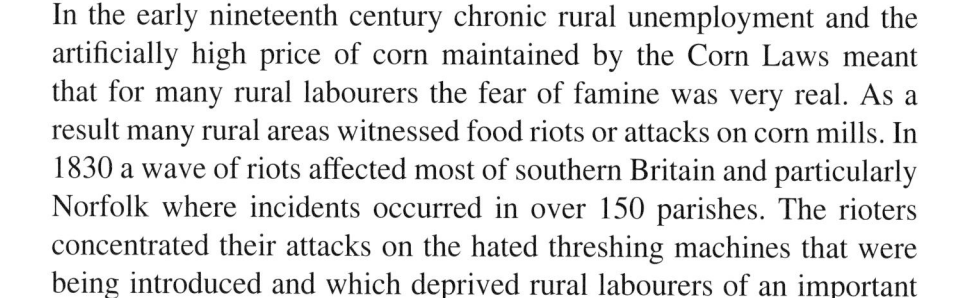

In the early nineteenth century chronic rural unemployment and the artificially high price of corn maintained by the Corn Laws meant that for many rural labourers the fear of famine was very real. As a result many rural areas witnessed food riots or attacks on corn mills. In 1830 a wave of riots affected most of southern Britain and particularly Norfolk where incidents occurred in over 150 parishes. The rioters concentrated their attacks on the hated threshing machines that were being introduced and which deprived rural labourers of an important source of winter employment - the hand flailing of cereal crops.

Farmers cut their demands for labour still further as parish rates rose to pay for poor relief. But lack of political rights put effective action out of the workman's reach. He could only resort to crime (theft, poaching, smuggling), or blackmail (incendiarism, machine-breaking) to force farmers to pay more. A new Act in 1816 made even suspected poachers liable to transportation to Australia. But between 1820 and 1830, per capita expenditure on the poor was actually reduced by almost one-quarter, by substituting money for a dole of bread.

Crime therefore increased even further (except after a good harvest, like that of 1827/28).

The following gives an idea of what life for the farm labourer in Norfolk was like under these conditions, and how the Squire of the nearby Shotesham Park Estate, Mr Robert Fellowes took responsibility for his workers.

TO THE
Labouring Poor of Shotesham,
Employed by Mr. Fellowes.

I have called you together to-day because I have heard with great concern that a spirit of discontent and dissatisfaction has lately arisen amongst some of you. I hear that a great many of you have lately attended some very tumultuous meetings, but I do not mean to enquire who attended them from compulsion, or who made choices as I wish to forget what is past, and to tell you what I mean to do in the future. In the first place I mean to encourage those who behave well. and to discourage those who behave ill – upon this I am determined – and whatever workman of mine shall from this time attend any illegal meeting, shall not only be discharged, but if the Laws of the Country have been violated, I will do my best endeavour that he shall be punished. Now, remember that I have said, as I shall be as good as my word. Next to Wages;-So long as the present price of Corn continues, I have ordered my Steward to pay every able-bodied man Two Shillings per day, whether he is married or single, as I think every man is worthy of his hire, and I have desired the taken-work to be put out at such a price that an industrious good-working man may be able to earn full Two Shillings per day, as I do not wish any man employed by me to go to the Poor Rate for Relief, except in very urgent cases. My Steward is present to hear what I say, and these are the directions I have given him ; but I have also positively ordered that the first man who misbehaves himself shall be immediately discharged, and I will never employ him again. I am afraid that some of you will now earn so much money, that you will be induced to neglect your work – if you do so, without leave or satisfactory reason, I have ordered you to be cut off Half-a-Crown for every day that you are absent. This is only fair, as otherwise you deprive another man of work. And here I must tell you that I met my Tenants yesterday, and I have the satisfaction to say that they have no just cause of complaint either of their Rents of their Tithes, but they say that the proposed increase of wages would press heavily upon them, and therefore I have determined to place all the Poor employed either by me or my Tenants upon the same footing and to pay the difference out of my own pocket. I hope that you will now think that the pledge which my Brother gave you last week has been most fully redeemed.

I wish to have about me a happy, contented, industrious Peasantry, and no exertions shall be wanted on my part to make you so. The Rents of your Cottages are now low, you have all good Gardens, and when sickness visits you, I believe your wants are well attended to, particularly those who have families, and as soon as the Law allows I immediately established a Brewery, solely for your benefit, so that every poor man might have a good wholesome Beer at the cheapest possible rate, and if I can make any alteration in the sort of Beer brewed, more conducive to your comfort, I am most ready to do so, as it is my hearty wish to see every poor man take his Bottle of Beer to his daily labour.

I shall soon be amongst you again, and shall then hope to hear a good report of you all; and I must again repeat that I am determined to give every encouragement to those who behave well, and to set my face firmly against those who behave ill.

Now Farewell,
ROBERT FELLOWES
Shotesham, December 7, 1830.

1831 – 1849
William Sancroft Holmes

John and Anne's eldest child, William Sancroft Holmes (b. 1815, d. 1849), became Justice of the Peace & D.L for the County of Norfolk in 1847.

He married Hester Elizabeth Gilbert (b. 1818), youngest daughter of Davies Gilbert of Eastbourne on 13th February 1840 in Lewes, Sussex. They had five children; Mary Anne (b. 1840 in Florence, Italy British Subject), Catherine (b. 1842), Hester (b. 1843), Alicia Charlotte (b. 1846) and John (b. 1847).

William Sancroft Holmes died on 11th September 1849 in Berne, Switzerland.

1849 – 1869
Hester Sancroft Holmes

William Sancroft Holmes' widow Hester inherited the Estate from her husband in 1849 and continued living there until her son John took over as Lord.

In 1864, a written description was found of the aforementioned 17th Century silver watch made by David Ramsay, the description was compiled by Rev A M Hopper for the Norfolk and Norwich Archaeological Society dated 1864. It was a handwritten document on light-blue note paper with an embossed heading; *"Gawdy Hall, Harleston, Norfolk"*. It accompanied photographs of the outer casing and dial of the watch by Cleer S Alger of Diss (local photographers of the time).

1869 – 1920
John Sancroft Holmes

The only son of William and Hester, John Sancroft Holmes was documented as being Lord of the Manor in 1869. He was Lt. Col. for the Prince of Wales Own Norfolk Artillery Militia. He was also Chairman of the Central Tea Company of Ceylon Ltd, Chairman of the Glendor Rubber Co. Ltd and Chairman of the Jorehaut Tea Co. Ltd.

In 1881 he was Justice of the Peace for the County of Norfolk, and was also Justice of the Peace and D.L. for the County of Suffolk. He was president of the Norfolk Chamber of Agriculture and of the Royal Norfolk Agricultural Association.

On 19th April 1869 John Sancroft Holmes was admitted to the Inner Temple, and in 1908 was Chairman of Magistrates. Between 1912 and 1920 he was Chairman of Norfolk County Council.

On 1st February 1877 John Sancroft Holmes married Edith Kingscote (b. 1850, d. 1937).

He laid the foundation stone of St John's Church in Harleston, a grand replacement to the little chapel in Harleston marketplace. The site of St John's Church was donated by William Martin Hazard within the grounds of his Caltofts estate (one of the previous owners of Caltofts was Tobias Frere, who also owned the Gawdy Hall Estates in the 1600s). In 1912, John's wife Edith opened the adjacent King George's Hall.

In 1878 extensive restoration work was carried out to Gawdy Hall, including the addition of the building running along the south side of the house, which remains today. Above the arch entrance is the Sancroft Holmes coat of arms.

The British Census Household Record for Gawdy Hall in 1881:-

John Sancroft HOLMES
Head, Male, age 33
Caroline FOSDICK
Servant, age 34 from Stokesby, Norfolk – Cook
Emma EVERITT
Servant, age 27 from Mendham, Suffolk – Housemaid
Ellen HOLLAND
Servant, age 19 from Denton, Suffolk – Housemaid
Lilly Short KING
Servant, age 17 from Pulham, Norfolk - Kitchen Maid
Charles HOWELL
Servant, age 16 from Alburgh, Norfolk - Page

On 28th June 1885, John's mother Hester Elizabeth was buried at Redenhall Church.

One morning in 1917, a military light plane crashed killing its Canadian pilot. Mrs Sancroft Holmes erected a cross near the spot on the Estate. A North American P-51D-15-NA Mustang came down on the edge of the Gawdy wood on June 21st 1945. Also during the Second World War, an RAF fighter shot down a German aircraft, which crashed into the wood. The German pilot was interred at Starston village churchyard. Many years after the war, the German pilot's remains were exhumed and returned to Germany. The German aircrew that bailed out were captured as POW in the village on the outskirts of Harleston.

The Germans made several raids by aircraft to attack and bomb Pulham airfield, and they did bomb and hit the big airship hangar on one occasion.

South side, 1901

East front, 28th September 1905

West view, 28th September 1905

1920 – 1937
Edith Sancroft Holmes

John Sancroft Holmes died at Gawdy Hall on 3rd August 1920. His widow Edith lived on at the Hall until her death on 8th November 1937. Edith and John did not have any children.

Above: Edith Sancroft Holmes with her two dogs.
Below: A picture post card taken of the Hall in May 1920.

1938 – Present Day
The Tresfon Family

In 1938 silver from the Estate was auctioned at Sotheby's. Among the items sold were the aforementioned silver watch, which fetched £460, and the two apostle spoons; one was Elizabethan and sold for £78, the other was Charles I and fetched £32.

The Estate was then sold in two auctions, and in the first about half the Estate lands were sold.

The second auction was held on 3rd September at the Royal Hotel, Norwich which consisted of 20 lots including the Hall and the Estate dwellings and was bought by Mr Jean Henri Tresfon for £37,005.

Born in June 1893 in Rotterdam, Holland, Mr Jean Henri Tresfon later became a naturalised British citizen. He spent much of his early working life with the Dutch margarine company Vandenberg, and was later closely connected with the merger between the Dutch company of Uni & Co and Lever Bros. He was a senior executive with Unilever, as the combined companies became known, before retiring in his mid 30s. Retirement, however, did not suite the astute business man and in 1935 Mr Tresfon joined Boulton & Paul as Managing Director. In 1934 Boulton & Paul employed 820 people, had a turnover of less than £½ million and made a pre-tax loss of £1,854. In 1968, the year prior Mr Tresfon retiring as Chairman and joint Managing Director, there were over 3,000 employees, a turnover exceeding £12 million and a profit of £1,189,000.

His involvement with Boulton & Paul in Norwich necessitated a move from his existing home in Hertfordshire to somewhere a little closer, hence the purchase of the Gawdy Hall Estates, lying just 15 miles south of the city.

Detailed below is the description of the Hall made for the auction in 1938 by Auctioneers Arnold, Son & Hedley of 9, Prince of Wales Road, Norwich:-

A most delightful typical Norfolk Moderate sized Moated Country Mansion known as

"Gawdy Hall"

On all fronts are stepped gables with shaped and moulded finials at apex and springing. The chimneys are handsome being in coupled or grouped shafts and the windows being modern in design with hood moulds over the head.

The Hall is approached by a front entrance drive over the Park, which leads to the east main front which has a spacious forecourt enclosed by a moulded brick panelled dwarf wall.

The front porch stepped gable opens into the magnificent

Reception Hall
with oak flooring (40-ft by 21-ft 6-ins) being panelled from floor to ceiling and having dado with carved modillioned cornice. The doorways and fireplace have on either side Ionic and Corinthian Columns. The open fireplace is with a heavy cast iron Sussex back and is enriched with a carved and moulded Mantel;

The Reception Room

On the south side of the Hall is a

Spacious Dining Room
(29-ft 9-ins by 22-ft) with oak flooring, open fireplace with delicate Adam design basket grate;

At the north end of the Hall is the
Billiard Room
(30-ft by 22-ft), the walls having raised and moulded panels from the

floor to a moulded and dentilled cornice. The open fireplace has en riched cast iron cheeks and back and is framed with a moulded and carved mantelpiece of the mid 18th century design ;

The Drawing Room
(22-ft 3-ins by 20-ft 3-ins) with oak flooring and bay shuttered window overlooks the west garden; there is a tiled hearth and sides with marble mantelpiece;

At the south end of the Main Hall and approached from the Side Entrance Hall is the

Library
(25-ft 3-ins by 19-ft 6-ins) which is panelled from floor to ceiling, capped with a bold cornice, it has a fine open fireplace with iron Sussex back;

Adjoining is

The Study
(15-ft 3-ins by 10-ft 9-ins) with tile stove and strong room in the south side with Milner's fireproof door;

Leading from the Main Hall is the magnificent

Main Staircase
of ample proportions, is of oak, the wide stairs having a balustrade of delicately moulded and twisted balusters (three to each step), the lighting is from a handsome Venetian window with Ionic columns and is completed with a unique elliptical shaped coffered dome;

This leads to

SEVEN PRINCIPAL BEDROOMS
five Dressing Rooms, two Bathrooms, two W.C.'s, nine Servants' Bedrooms, Bathroom and Airing Cupboard, W.C. ; as follows:-

The Green Bedroom
(22-ft by 20-ft) with fine old carved mantelpiece, inset cupboard;

In a self-contained two-roomed suite is the

Buff Bedroom
(21-ft 6-ins by 20-ft 3-ins), handsome fireplace with marble mantel and cupboard.
Small Bedroom adjoining (14-ft by 9-ft 3-ins);

Also communicating with the north Landing is a second suite of rooms comprising

The Mulberry Bedroom
(25-ft 3-ins by 20-ft 3-ins) with handsome marble mantelpiece.
Small Room (16-ft by 7-ft) with open fireplace. Mulberry Dressing Room (16-ft by 13-ft)

At the north end of the Main Corridor is the

Oak Bedroom
(17-ft 6-ins by 17-ft) finely panelled throughout from floor to ceiling with well-designed mantel and iron grate.
Small Dressing Room communicating

The Beach Bedroom
(17-ft 6-ins by 16-ft) with tiled stove and 2 windows each with window seat;

Alcove Bedroom
(18-ft by 13-ft 6-ins) which contains an arch supported by detached columns, of the Doric order - a tiled stove and window seat.

Small Bathroom with bath (H and C) and another Bathroom (13-ft 6-ins by 11-ft 9-ins) with bath (H and C);

South Bedroom
(22-ft by 16-ft 4-ins) with tiled and stone mantelpiece – communicating is a Dressing Room (13-ft 9-ins by 13-ft 9-ins) with stone mantelpiece and inset cupboard;

Along the South Landing are

Two Servants' good Bedrooms
(18-ft 6-ins by 17-ft) and (13-ft 6-ins by 12-ft), Housemaids' Cupboard with glazed sink (H and C) and W.C., Bathroom (H and C);

between the Ground and First Floors are

Two Bedrooms
facing south and a Linen Airing Cupboard;

On the second floor approached by two staircases are

Five Servants' Bedrooms
With easy access and very convenient for the Dining Room are the

DOMESTIC OFFICES

which include:-

Kitchen
(22-ft by 16-ft) with double oven Eagle Range and hot plate, large slate slab and painted dresser;

Scullery
with 2 glazed sinks, pump, a Beeston Domestic Independent Boiler for the hot water supply to Baths and domestic use – a brick oven and copper

Three larders with white glazed tiles to walls and a large Dairy with blue star slabs and white tile surrounds to walls, and stick house;

Butler's Pantry
with glazed sink (H and C), a green baize lined silver cupboard, dresser and cupboards over;

Housekeeper's Room
with fireplace and stone mantelpiece, storeroom and a

Servants Hall
with stone mantelpiece and curb and large painted cupboard;

Wine Cellar
with twelve wine bins, and a coal house adjoining;

Laundry
with row of washing tubs, iron copper, slow combustion stove and long ironing table and airing rack, large coal house.

The Mansion is efficiently heated on the ground and first floors by radiators from a Britannia Boiler at the north end of the house.

The lighting throughout is by electricity produced from a private plant as described in the Engine House.

A Permutit Water Softener is in the Garage block. The main Drainage system is across the Park.

On the west side of the Mansion and approaching the side entrance through a small iron gateway are the most attractive

PLEASURE GARDENS
with Lawns, bounded on the west and south sides by the Moat. Here is a Rose Garden in the centre of which is a marble sundial surrounded by a fine Juniper: on the north side is an old beech hedge:

The Old World Kitchen Gardens
are enclosed on three sides by a fine red brick wall and on the south side by clipped yew hedges with a beech archway in the centre. On the east and west sides are wall apple and plum trees and abutting upon the north wall is a row of half span

Glass Houses
comprising Peach House (40-ft by 22-ft), two Vineries (40-ft by 22-ft in all);

Greenhouse (20-ft by 22-ft) and a Coal House approximately (22-ft by 22-ft);

The houses are fitted with staging and are heated by a sectional Robin Hood Boiler;

There are also sunk-heated tomato, melon and cucumber houses and a row of nine cold frames.

A central walk with espalier fruit trees on either side leads through these gardens to herbaceous borders and yew hedges and running along the south end is rustic trellis work with rambler roses.

A row of Brick and Slate

Store Sheds
with apple racks, potato bins and shelves, and two open sheds. The Gardens are fully stocked with fruit trees and bushes and the borders are bedded with herbaceous plants of nearly every description.

Unfortunately, by the time Mr Tesfon bought the Estate, the roof of the Hall was in desperate need of repair. Quotations received however, far exceeded the purchase price, and along with severe taxes imposed at the time, the decision was made in 1939 to demolish the Hall.

The following is an excerpt from an article printed in a local newspaper at the time:-

"GAWDY HALL, HARLESTON
Mansion to be Demolished

Gawdy Hall near Harleston, for many years the home of the late Mr. John Sancroft Holmes, is to be demolished and the work has already begun. To many in the Harleston district and others further afield, the news has been received with regret, Harleston, in particular, having had long and happy associations with this typical country mansion. Originally an Elizabethan house, it was built shortly before 1568 and restored and faced in 1878. Following the death of Mr. Holmes' widow in November, 1937, fears were expressed that the estate as a whole might suffer from the heavy burdens of estate duties, and it caused little surprise when, on the instructions of Major E. Knatchbull-Hugessen, the Gawdy Hall estate, expending in all over 2428 acres, was split up and offered for sale last year by public auction. Few, however, thought that the mansion would eventually fall into the hands of housebreakers. A modern residence has recently been erected facing the park, and within a stone's throw of the hall. Panelling and oak floors have already been removed. The work of demolition is being carried out by Mr. Herbert Blackburn, of Harleston.

The original building probably formed three sides of a square, the fourth being closed by a wall and gate, and the north wing is believed to have contained a chapel. The famous brass double-headed eagle lectern at Redenhall Church is reputed to have been found in a moat at Gawdy Hall."

In its place an unusual and interesting house was built out of Red Deal, Columbian Pine and the external walls clad with Western Red Cedar, the floors and stairs of Burma Teak. It has a steeply pitched roof covered in Norfolk pantiles and features Dormer windows. The design of the house was evolved by Mrs Tresfon in collaboration with the chief architectural staff at Boulton & Paul, Mr R G Holmes. The unusual design brought the attentions of The Ideal Home and Gardening Magazine who published an extensive article in their February 1941 issue and also County Life who produced a similar article in their magazine on 13th April 1945.

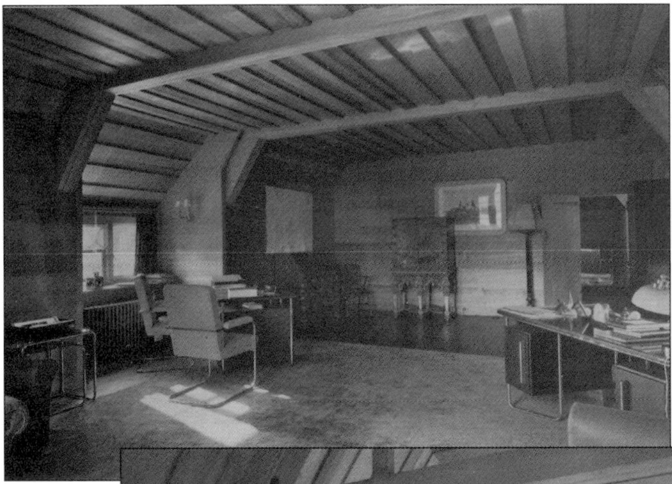

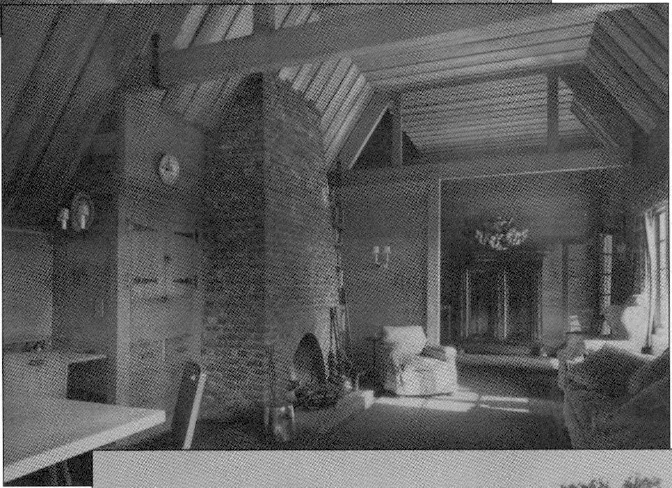

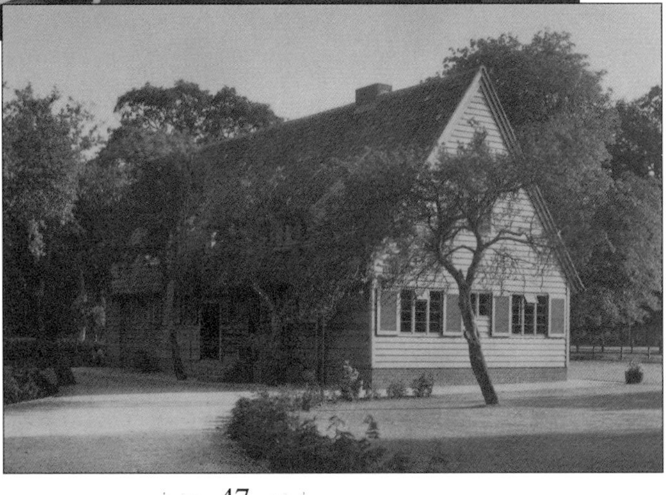

It was always the intention of Mr Tresfon that a significant house would be built on the site of the original Hall, but he enjoyed living in the new home so much, he considered it unnecessary.

In 1954 flowers and plants grown in the walled garden for Boulton & Paul's stand at the Norfolk Show brought in over £100, and there were also substantial sales of produce. However, although the gardens did bring in a minor source of income and it supplied the owners with fresh produce, it was predominantly used for pleasure.

Rows of potatoes were planted between the trees in the apple orchard, and there were also asparagus, rhubarb and artichoke beds. The vegetable plots, which have since been laid to grass, were not kept separate from the flower beds, in fact amongst the vegetables, flowers of every kind would be grown. At one point in recent history, the garden had over 1,500 roses as well as six vegetable plots, large fruit cages - which included 300 strawberry plants, and of course the glass houses, previously mentioned, which housed peaches and vines. The heated tomato, melon and cucumber houses were dismantled in the early '70s, but the large greenhouse running the length of the north wall remains today.

Although the peaches and vines have now gone, today's visitor is met by the delicious scent of climbing geraniums upon entry.

The walls of the garden continue to give shelter to many trees growing against them such as figs, gages and plums.

The garden before the vegetable plots were grassed over.

Some of the espalier trained apple and pear trees, which line the pathways in the garden, are now around 150 years old.

There are approximately 300 peonies contained in one bed, which are around forty years old and give a spectacular display in early Summer.

Gardener John Spurdens whose expertise is preserving this historic garden.

Farming Operations on the Estate in the Mid 20th Century

At the 1938 auction, the Gawdy Hall Estate consisted of five farms, small holdings, cottages and land totalling 1,050 acres, growing a wide variety of arable crops, alongside mixed livestock production. Mr Paul Seligman, the manager of the Estate from 1947 to 1989 sent monthly reports to the owners in South Africa and much of the information accompanying the following photographs, supplied by Mr Alan Oakley (who worked on the Estate between 1952 and 2002) has been gleaned from this fascinating source.

Drilling

Seed bed preparation – Alan Oakley driving a Fordson Major with mounted Triple K spring-tine and set of drag harrows. The harrows would probably have been thrown onto the spring-tine for moving from field to field. Dennis Revell is in the background with his lorry. All the Ford tractors at this time were purchased from JJ Wright of Dereham.

Danny Sheldrake driving an International Farmall H with set of drag harrows which is engaged in either pulling down or harrowing in after the drill. Conditions are obviously dry at the time as shown by the dust the harrows are producing.

Two men are loading seed corn and Fisons Compound fertiliser into a Massey Harris combine drill. Dougie Harper is holding the bushel hod next to George Flatt. They may well have treated the seed corn at the time with a mercury-based powder dressing against pests like wireworm – a highly hazardous operation by today's standards!

This operation involved two men - Jack Leeder is on the tractor, with Arthur O'Connor on the drill making sure the corn and fertiliser in the hoppers did not run out, and watching for blocked coulters.

Ernie Whiting driving a Fordson Dexta drilling sugar beet with Webb five-row mounted drill.

Harvest in the Fifties

It is interesting to note that even after the combine came to Gawdy Hall in the '40s, extensive use was still made of the threshing drum – very few farms owned a combine harvester at this time.

In 1954, as a result of *"seven weeks of the most unsettled weather for many years"*, the Estate bought its second new Diesel combine and sold its older petrol-engined model to Mr Andrews of Mill Farm, Alburgh for £725 *"a very fair price"*. It appears that the winter oats were cut with a binder and left standing in the field, but the spring oats were combined direct. Harvest peas were threshed from the tripods upon which they had been left to dry on the vine, using one of the combines. The vines would have been pitch-forked into the combine by hand, the reel probably having been removed for the purpose. The wheats were cut with a binder and stacked and were to be left until later in the winter for threshing. At the time, millers were paying from 18/- to 20/- (90p - £1) per cwt (50kg), as against the guaranteed price of 28/10d (c£1.45) fixed by the government, who would make up the difference! The malting barley grown on the heavier land was making 100/- per qr (£5) and feeding barley was making 80/- to 85/- (£4.00 to £4.25).

Three Fordson Majors and a Ransomes threshing drum were involved in the threshing operation - and ten men! (Not including the youngsters who were probably happily catching the rats that emerged from the diminishing stack). In the background can be seen an International B-450, dating the photograph to 1958 at the earliest. (Clockwise from top left; Isaac Garnham, Tom Denny, Arthur O'Connor, Dougie Harper, Alan Oakley, Norman Buck, Paul Seligman, Jack Leeder, Stanley Sheldrake and Charlie Allen).

Note the unguarded drum belt waiting to grab an unwary soul! The Fordson in the foreground is carting away filled sacks of grain with a buck-rake – a useful aid as a sack of wheat would probably have weighed at least 100kg. (Clockwise from top right – standing in the drum; Alan Oakley, Stanley Sheldrake, Charlie Allen, Jack Leeder on his tractor, Isaac Garnham and Tom Denny).

Here, one of the Fordsons is baling the straw emerging from the rear of the threshing drum, using a Massey Harris pick-up baler, which was new in May 1952. Records mention *"the string tying mechanism giving a considerable amount of trouble"*. The atmosphere was so full of dust and chaff that an extended air intake has been fitted to the tractor and an old sack hung over the radiator to stop it getting blocked. The man with the dirtiest job in threshing can be seen to the far left bagging off the chaff and calder. Not quite so bad with wheat or oats, when threshing barley he would be covered from head to foot in awns – little needle-like, intensely irritating, particles that stuck in clothes, and got inside collars and up sleeves! As the load on the trailer to the far right (almost out of picture) gets higher, two men with pitch-forks have joined forces to load the bales. (Clockwise from top left; Alan Oakley, Paul Seligman (can just see his head and shoulders behind the baler), Sam Bicker and George Stammers loading a bale onto the trailer, Tom Ransome standing just behind the Fordson, feeding the straw out of the drum into the baler).

It is interesting to see from the records that during the harvest of 1953, the Estate employed 58 men, all earning an average wage of £6/-/- per week. With the use of bigger and more efficient machinery, today there are just three men working a greater acreage.

In October and November 1954, records show that because of a succession of heavy rainstorms, field-work almost ground to a halt and the Estates crawler tractor – a Fowler VF, new in October 1951 – was taken off ploughing with a four-furrow trailer plough and used to pull the sugar beet trailer in the field, the single row harvester being powered by the largest of the Estates wheeled tractors, an International Farmall M – interesting because it was a 1940s tractor which had at some point been fitted with a Perkins Diesel engine. A contemporary newspaper article featuring the Gawdy Hall Estates harvester states that *"A dozen skilled farm-workers couldn't keep pace with a mechanical marvel like this ..."* Incidentally, one of the Fordson Major Diesels suffered from punctures at the same time, and muck carting was reduced to the horse and tumbril method, leaving the heaps to be spread (probably by hand) when the crawler was once again available to plough it in. A comment is made that the new hydraulic loader has speeded up the muck operation considerably!

Stanley Burlingham is shown here driving the International and Stanley Sheldrake on the Fowler.

When bought in 1951, the Fowler was chosen in preference to an Allis Chalmers crawler, also tried at the time, because the latter had difficulty in pulling the existing four-furrow plough or the digger plough with sub-soilers at an acceptable speed.

A rear view of the harvesting outfit shows why the crawler tractor was necessary in wet conditions – a loaded four wheeled turn-table trailer was too much for the wheeled tractors. Another job for the crawler in a wet time was carting felled timber out of the woods.

In the previous picture, George Stammers, Dougie Harper and Cyril Harper are off-loading the beet onto a railway truck at Harleston station. There was no time for slacking, it had to be unloaded before the next one arrived. In the 1948/9 season, 144 railway trucks were loaded in this manner. They held around 10 tonnes each.

Later the beet was carted by the Estates own Bedford lorry. Here it is being loaded at the clamp by means of a Cooks petrol-engined elevator.

Each year during January and February, between 1 and 1 ½ acres were cut out of the Gawdy Big Wood. This thinning out operation included cutting broaches and stakes for pea sticks and bean poles, faggotts, pergola poles for the roses in the gardens and linen props. They were all brought back to Abbey Yard for sawing, storing and pickling. The mature oak trees were lifted by crane onto a railway truck at the front of the wood shed, the truck was then pulled through the barn on the railway line which ran from the front to the back.

An electric generator with a pulley wheel drove huge saw blades inside the shed. A hook was hammered into one end of the trunk, which was then attached to a chain on the pulley. As the trunk was pulled slowly through, the saw cut the required thickness. Pegs were then placed in the cut as the saw drove through to hold the shape and to stop the wood from nipping the saw blades as they cut further into the trunk, until the two halves emerged from the shed at the back. The trunks were cut with amazing accuracy into any size and for any purpose, including all the maintenance work carried out on the Estate or to sell in Harleston.

Also during the winter months, general tidying was carried out around the Estate. Here a fairly major hedge cutting operation is in progress. A Fordson Dexta (driven by Ernie Whiting) is fitted with a mounted circular saw type hedge cutter, the saw being driven by its own petrol engine. Some effort has been made to guard the belt, but this is probably to keep falling hedging off it rather than for the operators safety – in this instance, Cyril Harper! Mention is made in October 1952 of a *"New hedge cutting machine"* – possibly this one as it appears to pre-date the Dexta. Prior to that in February 1952 a mechanical hedge cutter was hired in, which *"does not do the job quite as tidily as it can be done by hand, but it certainly saves a lot of time!"*

In January 1949 the manager's report states that *"one of the old Standard Fordson tractors was sold to Knights for £25 after we had exchanged various parts to put another into really good order. I am now trying to get £75 for the first of the Majors, but the demand for second-hand tractors, especially Fordsons, is very poor."*

In February 1949 the oldest Fordson E27N 'Major' was sold for £75 and in April another of the Fordson E27Ns was beginning to show signs of wear and an attempt was made to sell it, but a suitable offer was not forthcoming. Eventually Knights of Harleston offered to take it in part-exchange for a reconditioned International W4, originally priced at £360. After negotiations, this was reduced to £325, less £175 for the Fordson and £25 for a small pitch-pole harrow. Amongst other advantages, the fuel consumption of the International was expected to be almost exactly half of that of the Fordson – a saving of about £50 a year. The last remaining E27N was sold in July 1950, for £60.

In the same year Durrants were appointed to auction off some store cattle, 4 horses and surplus machinery consisting of the Allis Chalmers combine, baler, binder, Smythe drill, tractor plough, sheep equipment and baled straw. At the sale, on 23rd May, these are some of the prices realised. The Allis Chalmers combine made £250, the Deering binder made £150, the Smythe drill made £95 and a total of £140 was realised for the 4 horses. The combine was replaced by a new Massey Harris, which cost £995 in 1949. For the 1948 harvest, a Massey Harris combine had been hired from the War Agricultural Committee and was returned on September 10th.

In July 1950 a second Massey Harris combine was bought at a cost of £1,200, and in August, as harvest had progressed very well the older one was sold. It would *"have had to undergo a thorough overhaul to ensure trouble-free operation throughout another season. The very first reply we received to our advertisement lead to the immediate sale of the combine for £900, only ten percent less than the original purchase price!"*

In December 1950 one of the Caterpillar tractors was sold for £800, and a Farmall M bought at auction for £150.

The Estate entered into a contract with Birds Eye Foods Ltd in January 1952, for the growing of 30 acres of green peas for freezing. They were to be delivered to a vining plant near Flixton Hall, the stripped vines being returned to be made into silage.

Livestock on The Estate

The herd of Red Polls, a traditional Norfolk/Suffolk breed was started shortly after the arrival of the new owners and was kept in the Home Farm buildings (the buildings which back onto the gardens). In June 1952, *"rapid deterioration of the grazing resulted in a considerable drop in milk yields"*. In May the daily average was 45 gallons, June was 37.5 gallons. Two barren heifers were sold for a total of £124.5.7d plus one cow, Combs Sweet Rosamund 7th who was just over 13 years old, weighing 12 cwts (nett) and had produced 11 calves. She was graded 'A+'.

There were originally 25 milkers kept on the park, and calves that were produced gradually increased the numbers. One of the heifers was taken to the Smithfield Show in London where it won a rosette. But as time went by, unless the Estate stepped up the numbers, there was not enough revenue to be made in this venture. Not wanting to add to the herd, which would make more and more mess around the park, the herd was disposed of in the late '50s.

Another traditional local breed were the Suffolk sheep kept on the arable parkland with their diet supplemented by sugar beet tops produced elsewhere on the Estate. Unfortunately this breed is prone to 'Scrapey' - an irritating skin disease, which causes the animals to rub themselves against whatever they can find to ease the irritation, but of course in the process, scratching off valuable wool.

They were replaced by Scotch half-bred which were a border/Leicester cross and were not prone to the same ailment as the Suffolks and also did not need the additional sugar beet in their diet and grazed happily all year round on the parkland.

The farming of pigs started with a single large black sow, kept at Oaklands Farm, which was crossed with a large white boar, and from this first litter began the successful pig business. The Estate adapted the buildings at North Lodge for a second herd. Large pens with concrete troughs were made in the Starston farm buildings and an area of seven acres was fenced in at Lodge Farm where there was also a farrowing unit to oversee all the new litters. Of course Boulton & Paul supplied all the troughs, field sheds, feed bins and wire netting.

In June 1952 three litters of pigs, 28 in all, were born in the course of the month. A total of 23 pigs were sold as baconers at an average price of £22.18.0d each. During September of the same year, 60 piglets were born, but 4 died shortly after birth. 18 (2 young gilts and 16 baconers) were sold at an average price of £21.15.7ad each.

Poultry on the Estate was also big business. About 10 enclosures, roughly the size of half a tennis court, each housed Boulton & Paul arks and were stocked with 60 pullets. In September 1952, as more and more of the pullets started laying, egg production reached 600 a day, the eggs being sold on contract to companies such as Ross. In the same month, 147 unproductive hens were supplied to Birds Eye Foods Ltd for £79.7.8d.

The growing trend however, was turning towards battery farming, which the Estate was not keen on following and so from the mid '60s they turned their expertise to broiler breeding.

Traditional Norfolk Black turkeys were also kept on the Estate together with geese, but they were mainly used for Christmas gifts, the most famous recipient being Sir Winston Churchill with whom Mr Tresfon formed a relationship during the Second World War as an economic advisor.

Mr Tresfon was also very good friends with Sir Arthur 'Bomber' Harris, one of the more controversial figures of WW2. Harris was in charge of the massive Allied air campaign against Nazi Germany from 1942 to 1945 causing countless civilian losses and enormous destruction, and has been a matter of contention ever since.

At the time of his death, Mr Tresfon owned over 35 companies, both in England and South Africa where his family still reside today.

The Estate has since been passed to Mr Tresfon's grand-sons, Jean Henri and Jacques Pierre Tresfon who currently live in South Africa.

Brief History of the Inner Temple

In the middle of the 12th century, the Military Order of the Knights Templar built a fine round church by the Thames, which became known as the Temple Church. Two centuries later, after the abolition of the Order in 1312, lawyers came to occupy the Temple site and buildings. They formed themselves into two societies, the Inner Temple and Middle Temple, first mentioned by name in a manuscript yearbook of 1388.

The medieval Inns of Court, which included Lincoln's Inn and Gray's Inn as well as the Inner Temple and Middle Temple, were organised on the same basis as the colleges at Oxford and Cambridge Universities, offering accommodation to practitioners of the law and their students and facilities for education and dining. The term 'Inns of Court' seems to have been adopted on account of the hospitality offered to those associated with the law courts. By the end of the 16th century, the Inns had largely developed into their present form, governed by an elected Treasurer and Council of Benchers, administered by a salaried Sub-Treasurer and his staff.

The majority of students were the sons of country gentlemen, not intended for the legal profession. The minority who dedicated themselves to in-depth study of the law were expected to keep the two learning vacations (Lent and Summer) each year, when courses of lectures were given on the old statutes, and also the more relaxed Christmas vacation, when a lord of misrule and his court presided over the festivities.

In term-time the students attended Westminster Hall, to watch the courts in action, and throughout the year they took part in lengthy, intricate moots. For these vocational exercises, the hall of each inn was arranged to resemble a court, with a bar and bench. A young student sat inside the bar as an 'inner barrister'; when he became suitably qualified to argue points of law, he was called to the bar, and as an 'outer barrister' stood outside the bar at moots. In due course a barrister would be expected to deliver a lecture (or 'reading'), after which he sat on the bench at moots as a 'bencher'. These degrees achieved public recognition in the sixteenth century; but they have remained to this day inns of court degrees, referring to the bar and bench of the inns rather than of the courts.

Sir John Soane, Architect

Sir John Soane (b. 1753, d. 1837), the son of a bricklayer, was an architect who specialised in the Neo-Classical tradition. During his studies at the Royal Academy, he won the Academy's silver medal (1772), gold medal (1776) and finally a travelling scholarship in 1777, which he spent on developing his style in Italy. He returned to England in 1780 and settled in East Anglia where he established a small architectural practice.

In 1788, he succeeded Sir Robert Taylor as Architect and Surveyor to the Bank of England, the exterior of the Bank being his most famous work. During his time in London, Soane ran a lucrative architectural practice, remodelling and designing country homes for the landed gentry. Among Soane's most notable works are the dining rooms of both numbers 10 and 11 Downing Street for the Prime Minister and Chancellor of Britain, the Dulwich Picture Gallery which is the archetype for most modern art galleries, and his country home at Pitzhanger Manor in Ealing.

Soane died in London in 1837 and is buried in a vault of his own design in the churchyard of Old St. Pancras Church.

Arms of Gawdy

Vert, a tortois passant ar.
Crest: A wolf passant, per pale, ar. and gu.